Obamacare *for Beginners*

OBAMACARE
for Beginners

GARAMOND
— PRESS —

Contents

Introduction

During the presidential election of 2012, Republican candidate Mitt Romney promised that on "day one" of his presidency he would repeal the Patient Protection and Affordable Care Act (PPACA), the health care reform bill signed into law by President Barack Obama on March 23, 2010, which came to be known as Obamacare. Some Republican candidates for Congress that year made similar promises. Meanwhile, supporters of President Obama, as well as some Democratic candidates for Congress, vowed that they would make sure Obamacare was preserved and implemented. Campaigners on both sides sometimes tried to cast the 2012 election as a referendum on health care reform.

It is little wonder that Obamacare has become such a lightning rod of controversy. In fact, not since President Lyndon Johnson signed the Civil Rights Act in 1968 has there been such turmoil over a piece of legislation in Washington, D.C. Cutting through all the rhetoric on both sides has not been easy. In this guide, we will look at how the legislation came about, what it actually says, the arguments for and against it, and how things might change for you as its provisions go into effect.

Understanding Obamacare

WHAT IS OBAMACARE?

Obamacare is a comprehensive overhaul of the health care insurance system, aimed primarily at ensuring that affordable health care is available to all Americans. It requires that everyone in the United States have health insurance. If individuals (citizens as well as resident aliens with green cards) wish to opt out, they will pay a tax penalty. The law promises to reduce health care and health insurance costs, which have risen sharply over the past decade, and make it possible for the working poor who don't receive health insurance benefits from their employers to purchase lower-cost insurance for themselves and their children. Americans who receive government assistance in the form of Medicare or Medicaid (see "Key Terms") probably won't see their benefits change.

IMPLEMENTING OBAMACARE

Obamacare is a complex law and few have actually read it in its entirety—including some lawmakers who voted for or against it—let alone understand all its ramifications. The law won't be fully implemented until 2020, but there are several milestones along the way. For example, children of insured parents were covered up to age 26 as of September 2010. At the same time, insurers were required to provide free mammograms and colonoscopies to their customers, meaning insured individuals weren't responsible for a co-pay for those tests. As of August 2012, insurers were required to provide free preventive care for insured women. By 2014, an individual mandate tax will be enforced, which means Americans who are not covered by health insurance will pay a penalty of up to $285 per year, depending on the person's income. That penalty will gradually increase until 2016, when the maximum will reach $2,085.[1] For a timeline of Obamacare milestones, see the "Obamacare Timeline" section.

A BRIEF HISTORY OF THE HEALTH CARE DEBATE IN THE UNITED STATES

Many industrialized nations offer universal health care (see "Key Terms"), a trend that grew after World War II. The United States, however, has adopted a private system, most often based on insurance provided by a person's employer. The reasons for this are complex. Some people believe American politicians in the mid-twentieth century feared that universal health care was a kind of socialism. They considered all forms of socialism an affront to the American way of life, which they believed was rooted in capitalism. Rather than embrace universal health care as a national good, they preferred to let market forces handle health care for employees. Others believe that powerful lobbies (insurance companies and medical professionals) want to protect their profits and have strongly influenced the debate from the beginning. The roots of these viewpoints can be found in early American history.

Early Twentieth Century

As early as 1911, Great Britain passed the National Insurance Act, which gave workers health insurance but did not cover their dependents. In 1901, Theodore Roosevelt, a Republican and a Progressive, was the first president to attempt to pass universal health care in the United States. The idea was met with resistance by others in government and went nowhere. President Franklin D. Roosevelt, a Democrat, also tried—and failed—on two occasions (1935 and 1939) to pass health care reform legislation, but because the country was in the throes of the Great Depression, other urgent issues facing Congress took precedence. Health care reform fell through the cracks. In 1943, the Wagner-Murray-Dingell Bill called for mandatory national health insurance and a payroll tax to fund it. The bill was met with opposition from the American Medical Association (AMA), a strong lobby in Washington, and was deemed too "socialist" for America.[2]

The '40s and '50s

President Harry S. Truman, FDR's successor and a Democrat, also attempted to pass a national health insurance bill. While FDR's plan had attempted to offer health care to the millions of poor, unemployed people, Truman's called for a universal health care reform affecting all Americans. But the onset of the Cold War again made the proposal seem to be part of a socialist agenda, and once again the bill met with opposition and died. Opponents included the AMA, which lobbied successfully to block it. Proponents of the plan included labor unions. In 1943, a nationwide Gallup poll found 59 percent of Americans favored the bill.[3]

In 1955, Republican President Dwight D. Eisenhower again asked Congress to pass a national health care bill.[4] Once again, the attempt failed.

The '60s, '70s, and '80s

President John F. Kennedy, a Democrat whose presidency was cut short when he was assassinated in 1963, was also an advocate of a universal health care plan. Once again, there was strong lobbying from the AMA against it, and hard lobbying for it from labor organizations, this time joined by senior citizens. Kennedy's successor, Democrat Lyndon B. Johnson, proposed an ambitious set of domestic programs he called the Great Society, which included plans to ensure all Americans could get medical care. Universal health care still met with strong resistance. However, in 1965 Johnson signed into law Medicare, addressing the medical needs of Americans age 65 and over, and Medicaid, which helps impoverished citizens through state programs subsidized by the federal government.

President Richard Nixon, a Republican and a proponent of health care reform, appealed to Congress to pass a national health care law. "One of the most cherished goals of our democracy is to assure every American an equal opportunity to lead a full and productive life," he said in a message to Congress in 1971.[5] His plan was not as comprehensive as his predecessors', but it met with the same fate. During his presidency, three attempts by Congress to pass a national health care bill failed.

Republican President George H. W. Bush, who opposed a universal health care plan, did propose a plan under which Americans could buy into Medicaid, but Congress didn't act on it.

The Clinton Presidency

The next attempt to pass a universal health care system in the United States came during Democratic President Bill Clinton's administration, when First Lady Hillary Rodham Clinton spearheaded the Health Security Act of 1993. The comprehensive reform plan for universal health care, which included a requirement for employers to provide coverage through carefully monitored health maintenance organizations (HMOs), was presented to Congress, where it ultimately died—due, in part, to lobbying by insurance and pharmaceutical companies. Hillary Clinton's plan shared many similarities with a plan Mitt Romney signed into law when he was governor of Massachusetts (2003–2007). The major differentiator, as Romney saw it, was state versus federal government control. Romney believed each state should decide for itself whether universal health care should be required, and if so, how it should be handled.

State Children's Health Insurance Program (SCHIP)

Although the Clinton health care reform agenda did not pass, a small state-federal partnership known as the State Children's Health Insurance Program (SCHIP) was voted into law in 1997. The bipartisan program was sponsored by Democratic Senator Edward Kennedy and Republican Senator Orrin Hatch. The program provided matching federal funds to states to cover uninsured children in families with modest incomes who earn too much to qualify for Medicaid. The program was authorized for ten years.

In 2007, as part of its reauthorization, both houses of Congress passed a bipartisan measure to expand SCHIP coverage. Republican President George W. Bush vetoed it, as well as a subsequent version, saying he believed the plan would "federalize health care." He did sign a basic extension of SCHIP through 2009. That year, Congress extended and expanded the scope SCHIP, funded by a tax on tobacco products.

ARGUMENTS FOR OBAMACARE

[Editor's note: The section "Arguments for Obamacare" is written from the perspective of an individual who supports Obamacare.]

The United States spends more per capita on health care than any other developed country, yet it is one of the few developed countries that lacks universal health care.[6] The debate over health care reform in this country is fraught with partisan strife that sometimes puts the profits of insurance companies, medical professionals, and medical institutions before the needs of ordinary Americans. Opponents argue that the United States cannot afford universal health care, yet other industrialized nations with smaller economies have been able to extend health care to all their citizens.

Obamacare does not provide universal health care. It does mandate near-universal health insurance coverage. The most obvious beneficiaries of Obamacare are the approximately thirty million employed Americans who currently are not receiving health insurance benefits. Obamacare also closes the gap in prescription medication coverage for senior citizens, ensures coverage for children, and offers tax rebates for small businesses that provide coverage to employees.

Health care insurers have increased their premiums to the point where millions of Americans can't afford insurance. The uninsured typically do not get any preventive care, and do not go to the doctor's office when they are sick. Instead, they rely on hospital emergency rooms, the last resort, when they are so ill that they must see a doctor. This ultimately drives up the cost of health care.

In the long run, Obamacare will drive down health care costs, as consumers will rely more on their general practitioners and won't use emergency rooms as walk-in clinics. Additionally, the need for health care providers and their support staff will increase, which will ultimately increase the number of Americans employed in the medical workforce.

While some segments of the population will be required to buy into Obamacare perhaps unwillingly, the program is set up so healthy adults 18 to 29 years old, many of whom typically do not buy health insurance because they do not need a lot of medical services, are required to purchase health insurance. As the pool of insured healthy people grows larger, they will balance out those who need more expensive care, such as older Americans and those with chronic ailments. The insurance companies will make enough money from their healthy customers to be able to keep premiums lower for everyone.

In addition to the individual mandate—the requirement that everyone must have health insurance—Obamacare also regulates insurers. They will be prohibited from denying coverage for pre-existing conditions (see "Key

Terms") or from charging seniors and women more, for example, and their profits will be limited. Free preventive care will drive down the number of people who seek health care only when it has become very expensive and/or it's too late to help them. Americans will be healthier, because early detection and treatment of many diseases is often the best medicine. In addition, the competition for new customers will help create a healthy competitive environment for health insurance. Companies may be prohibited from withholding expensive treatments from consumers, and may have to offer more and better services at more competitive prices.

ARGUMENTS AGAINST OBAMACARE

[Editor's note: The section "Arguments against Obamacare" is written from the perspective of an individual who opposes Obamacare.]

Requiring people to buy health insurance, whether they want it or not, is an infringement on personal rights and the freedom to choose how to spend their money. This requirement is known as the individual mandate (see "Key Terms"), and there are specific legal arguments that can be made against it. For example, all contracts require that both parties freely consent to sign them. If a contract is mandated, the law says it is unenforceable. In addition, while the Constitution gives Congress the power to regulate business activities (such as purchasing insurance) between states, it does not have the power to regulate activities within individual states. Opponents of the individual mandate say it therefore exceeds the power of the federal government.

There is also a fear that the already high cost of health care will continue to rise under this program, ultimately hurting the federal deficit. More people will become eligible for Medicaid, and more coverage will be mandated for Medicare patients. These increases will be paid for by cutting the reimbursements made to medical service providers, thus reducing the number of doctors, clinics, and hospitals that will accept Medicare and Medicaid patients, ultimately limiting those patients' access to heath care.

Less income, along with increased regulations for doctors pertaining to record-keeping and other office practices, will also act as a disincentive to enter the medical profession. There is already a shortage of doctors in the United States, and more patients, combined with fewer doctors, means the United States may face a serious doctor shortage in the coming years, which means long lines and longer waits for needed health care.

While health insurance premiums will go down for some people, they will rise for others—especially healthy young people, who will find themselves having to share the medical costs of the elderly and the chronically ill. More government regulation of the insurance industry will prevent market forces from acting in a way that naturally regulates prices in the marketplace.

With the country already facing a record-breaking fiscal deficit, the budgetary implications of expanding Medicaid and implementing mandatory coverage may be poorly understood. The Congressional Budget Office (CBO) predicts a small reduction in the federal deficit, but these are only projections and have been disputed. Additionally, the numbers issued by the CBO have steadily increased as Obamacare has gone through the process of debate, passage, and challenges. For example, the CBO initially stated that implementing Obamacare would result in a reduction in the federal deficit of $210 billion. However, revisions in both the act itself as well as continually rising health care costs have reduced the savings figure to $84 billion.[7] Moreover, an independent analysis of the CBO's forecast regarding the cost of the new health care system found that cost estimates have been understated. According to that analysis, the actual cost to the federal government will be up to five times higher than CBO estimates.[8]

PASSING OBAMACARE

Early in 2009, President Obama's first year in office, the president asked Congress to come up with a health care reform bill. Congress devoted a great deal of that session to discussing various alternatives. During the summer Congressional recess, politicians held town hall meetings in their local districts, explaining to their constituents why they were for or against health care reform. The town hall meetings were explosive, sometimes devolving into disruptive shouting matches and even violence.

Groups representing both sides of the argument actually instructed their supporters on how to either control or disrupt the discourse at these town hall meetings. Local people were sometimes crowded out by ardent supporters of one side or the other who traveled around the country seeking to make their point of view known. Some politicians resorted to virtual town hall meetings, by telephone or Internet, to avoid the drama.[9] As passions flared, informed discussion and debate sometimes seemed impossible.

Despite that chaotic summer, the House of Representatives passed a health care reform bill in November 2009. The following month, the Senate passed its own bill. In March 2010, the House abandoned its bill in favor of an amended version of the Senate bill. The votes largely followed party lines, although a handful of moderate Republicans voted with Democrats to pass the bill.

THE FUTURE OF OBAMACARE

Obamacare was challenged in the Supreme Court in 2012. The two main points of contention were the individual mandate and the expansion of Medicaid. In a five-to-four vote, the Supreme Court upheld the act.[10] As it is supposed to roll out gradually through 2020, though, several things can still happen along the way to change the language of the law. The next presidential election is in 2016, and there is a possibility that the new administration will try to repeal Obamacare or make substantial changes. By that date, many provisions of the act will already be in motion and the public will have a clearer picture of what implementation actually means.

However, because of the complexity of the act, some tweaks are inevitable. The bureaucracy alone of this mammoth law, which is currently detailed in a 2,500-page document, will likely need to be reduced. Updates to health care law will probably dovetail expected major changes in the health care industry, from the role of technology in medicine and data collection to a shift to disease prevention and personalized health care.

What Obamacare Means for You

The following are brief descriptions of how Obamacare will affect various groups of people.

INSURED AMERICANS

Typically, insured Americans receive health insurance from their employer (or through an employed family member) as a part of their benefits package. Others, mostly the self-employed, privately purchase individual insurance plans. Insurance plans can vary widely, depending on such variables as the size of the company, the coverage offered, and even the geographic location of the employer and/or the workers. Most insured Americans pay at least a portion of the cost of their insurance package, and this portion can also vary widely—again, based on many variables, including the percentage of the policy cost that is paid for by the employer and how many family members are also covered. Currently, most employers pay between 50 percent and 80 percent of the cost of a health benefits package,[11] while employees are expected to pay for the remainder for their coverage.

Before Obamacare

The American health care system typically works on a fee-for-service system. Every visit to a doctor or clinic generates a separate charge, in addition to diagnostic fees, such as laboratory and radiology charges. The insured party is usually responsible for a co-pay and sometimes an annual or lifetime deductible, and sometimes also for a part of the fees. Co-pays and deductibles vary widely, depending on the type of plan offered, and the insured may also pay more for out-of-network versus in-network providers. Some plans also contain "carve-outs" (e.g., maternity care), for which the insured party has to pay higher premiums if the coverage is desired.

With some exceptions, based on individual state laws, health insurance companies are the sole deciders of what they will and will not cover, and what services they will or will not pay for.

With Obamacare

After full implementation of Obamacare, there will be few changes for Americans already insured by their employers. There may be an initial small increase in premium costs for some people, but it is predicted that by 2020, when Obamacare is fully implemented, health care costs will start to drop, thus halting premium increases. The premium increases are expected to occur mostly in January 2014, when sweeping changes will take place in various programs. These changes will reflect the new coverage requirements set forth by the federal government, such as mandatory free preventive care and diagnostics, mammograms, colonoscopies, and screenings for HIV and other sexually transmitted diseases. Health insurance companies will also no longer be allowed to deny coverage for pre-existing conditions.

Proponents of the act point to these new guidelines, mostly in preventive care, as a way for the United States to reduce health care costs in the long run. Opponents warn that when the new requirements go into effect, insurance costs will rise to cover the newly mandated services.

UNINSURED AMERICANS

It is generally estimated that more than thirty million Americans are uninsured. A large number are employed but their employer does not offer health insurance. When unemployed people are also counted, the actual number of uninsured Americans is closer to forty-eight million. Many small businesses do not offer health insurance, and many hourly and part-time workers do not qualify in their company for this benefit. Self-employed people must purchase their own insurance, and many cannot afford it. Many uninsured people earn too much money to qualify for Medicaid but don't make enough to pay the high monthly premiums charged for individual policies. This group consists mostly of adults age 18 to 65, although in states with lower income requirements for Medicaid or SCHIP eligibility, there are also many uninsured children under the age of 18.

Before Obamacare

Uninsured Americans tend to seek their primary care from local hospital emergency rooms, which, with the passage of the Emergency Medical Treatment and Active Labor Act (EMTALA) in 1986, are prohibited from turning away patients, regardless of their ability to pay. Unpaid visits account for a large proportion of hospital financial deficits. Using hospitals in this way has also driven up the cost of health care; it is inefficient to use the extensive facilities of hospital emergency rooms for relatively minor health problems that could be treated in a doctor's office. In addition, studies show that regular preventive care is far less expensive in the long run than emergent or prolonged care. Many times, though, uninsured people feel they cannot afford preventive care and will not seek medical help until they are seriously ill.

With Obamacare

State Medicaid programs will be expanded in 2014 to accept all people whose income is at or below 133 percent of the federally designated poverty level.[12] The poverty level changes year to year.[13] People with incomes between 134 and 400 percent of the poverty level will be eligible for subsidies (given as a tax rebate) toward purchasing an insurance plan from one of the proposed health insurance exchanges, or HIX (see "Key Terms").

Each state is supposed to launch a HIX by 2014. Each HIX will be like a virtual insurance shopping mall, where each insurance company that wants to participate in the exchange will describe what they have to offer and consumers will be able to choose their health insurance plan. Each HIX will also provide the sole venue where members of Congress will get their health insurance. Insurance companies will have to meet certain federally mandated criteria for what is offered in their plans, including free preventive care. The insurance companies must offer four plan levels (Bronze, Silver, Gold, and Platinum). Plans with more and better coverage can be offered at a higher cost, but there will be caps on the pricing of the different plans. For those who qualify, government subsidies will be applied to all exchange plans, with the difference between the subsidy and the cost of the plan paid by the consumer.

Individual states can refuse to set up exchanges, at which point the federal government will run them. So far, eighteen states have committed to setting up an exchange, seventeen states have asked the federal government to run them, and the remaining states are looking to partner with the federal government to set up and run exchanges.[14]

Proponents of Obamacare state that with the expansion of Medicaid and the implementation of HIXes, more than thirty million Americans who are currently uninsured will have access to comprehensive health insurance. Covered preventive care will encourage people to seek medical care before an illness can become serious, thus reducing health care costs overall.

Opponents point to still-rising health care costs and say adding thirty million newly insured people to a system that requires a certain level of coverage will cause both the states' Medicaid programs and the private health care insurance companies participating in the exchanges to be overwhelmed, and that federal subsidies will do nothing more than increase the national deficit and provide more poorly overseen entitlement programs.

EMPLOYED AMERICANS

Many employed Americans currently receive health insurance from their employers as part of their benefits package. However, this tends to apply to only full-time employees working for relatively large employers. Historically, employers have not been required to offer health insurance as part of a benefits package, but many companies have used health care benefits as a way to attract and retain employees. Self-employed Americans must purchase individual plans, typically at a high cost, or go without health insurance. In professions with a large number of self-employed workers, self-employed Americans have sometimes formed groups or unions to increase their purchasing power and negotiate lower health insurance rates for their members. The Freelancers Union, a national group, is one such union that was formed primarily to provide benefit plans to its members at group rates.

Before Obamacare

Employees of larger companies typically receive some sort of health insurance coverage from their employers, although providing this coverage is not mandatory. How much they must pay for the coverage, what members of their family the insurance may also cover, and what type of coverage is provided are determined solely by the employer. Some companies with a large number of minimum-wage employees offer a minimal package called a mini-med plan (see "Key Terms"). These plans typically cover only a few primary care doctor visits per year and require beneficiaries to pay for prescriptions, diagnostic testing, and most, if not all, costs associated with a hospital stay or emergency room visits. Some companies offer health insurance to their full-time employees but not to part-time employees.

Many (although certainly not all) employees of smaller businesses, part-time employees, and minimum-wage employees, plus all self-employed persons, have had to either purchase individual plans (generally quite expensive), get health insurance through a family member whose employer does offer this benefit, or go without health insurance. Young adults (ages 18–29) who are no longer covered under their parents' plan typically do not regard obtaining health care insurance as a high priority, because they are usually healthy, and so also tend to go without coverage unless they receive health insurance through their employer. Roughly thirty million people are employed but uninsured. The pool is made up mostly of the self-employed, underemployed, or minimum-wage employees who do not qualify for state Medicaid benefits. States currently set their own Medicaid eligibility requirements, so people who might be accepted into one state's program may fail to qualify for another state's program.

With Obamacare

As of January 2014, if you work thirty hours a week or more, on average, and your employer has at least fifty full-time workers, they are required to offer you a health insurance plan or must pay a $2,000 fine per employee (not counting the first thirty employees). The insurance offered must cover at least 60 percent of the cost of benefits, and the employees' share may not be more than 9.5 percent of their income.[15] It will still be up to employers whether they wish to extend coverage to family members of the employee.

Eligibility for Medicaid coverage will be determined by the federal government: Anyone who earns 133 percent or less of the federally defined poverty level,[16] whether employed or not, will be accepted into their state's Medicaid plan. Persons earning between 134 and 400 percent of the federal poverty level will be eligible to purchase health care coverage from one of the state's exchanges, with a sliding-scale subsidy provided by the federal government through tax credits on an individual's income tax return. People who earn more than 400 percent of the poverty level are free to purchase an insurance plan from the HIX, but there will be no federal subsidies available for them. Most of the people earning more than 400 percent of the poverty level are expected to be covered on employer-offered plans.

Proponents argue that by implementing national standards, mandating health insurance coverage from employers, and expanding the states' Medicaid programs, the pool of uninsured Americans will be all but eliminated. Projections show that after full implementation in 2020, less than 3 percent of Americans will remain uninsured. The larger pool of insured persons should drive health insurance costs down, as the risk is spread more widely.

Opponents say the mandate on employers to provide health insurance will prove an onerous burden, especially for smaller businesses. They predict it will stifle economic growth by providing a disincentive for businesses to hire more people. They also warn that expanded Medicaid and new subsidy programs will soon become bloated entitlement programs that ultimately leave employer-based insurance policyholders and the American taxpayers footing the bill.

UNEMPLOYED AMERICANS

Today, unemployed Americans generally fall into one of four categories: they qualify for Medicaid; they are uninsured; they were previously employed and have extended their coverage under the Consolidated Omnibus Budget Reconciliation Act (COBRA) (see "Key Terms"); or they are covered under an employed, insured family member's plan. Usually, if a person receives unemployment benefits or has an employed family member, the income disqualifies him or her from Medicaid.

Before Obamacare

When covered employees lose their full-time jobs (most often, when employment is terminated), they are able to extend their health insurance under COBRA for themselves and any family members who were also covered. This coverage typically lasts eighteen months. The former employee must pay the entire cost of the health insurance premium, which means COBRA coverage costs a lot more than the typical payroll deduction for health insurance.[17]

When a person starts receiving unemployment benefits, this usually generates an individual income that is too high to qualify for Medicaid. However, unemployment benefits are low, making it expensive for an unemployed person or their family members to purchase an individual health insurance plan, or even to afford health insurance premiums under COBRA.

With Obamacare

After January 2014, when Medicaid programs expand and state insurance exchanges open, some unemployed people will qualify for Medicaid and some will be able to purchase a plan from their state's exchange with the help of a federal subsidy, even if they are receiving unemployment benefits. Others will remain dependent on their employed family member's insurance plan. COBRA will still be offered to the newly unemployed by their ex-employers, but it is projected that many people will opt for one of the states' exchange programs rather than pay the usually high cost of COBRA.

Proponents argue that by offering affordable health care plans to the unemployed, the period of time that a person is uninsured will be eliminated, or at least greatly reduced. This will lead, indirectly, to a reduction in overall health care costs in the United States, as well as provide a safety net for the newly unemployed who have chronic health issues.

Opponents point to continually rising health care costs, which, if not curbed, will drive up the cost of insurance plans, causing more out-of-pocket expenditures for people purchasing plans from the exchanges. They also argue that with an expanded Medicaid program, the amount of time doctors can spend with patients will be reduced and facilities that accept Medicaid patients will be overburdened.

PEOPLE RESIDING IN THE UNITED STATES WITHOUT LEGAL PERMISSION

Under Obamacare, people residing in the United States without legal permission, currently estimated at anywhere between seven million and twenty million,[18] will not be covered unless they can afford to purchase a private plan from an insurer. This does not mean, however, that they will have no access to health care. These immigrants will not be refused care at local emergency rooms, regardless of their ability to pay. Individual hospitals will have to absorb those expenses and may increase the charges on services provided to insured people to cover the losses.

YOUNG ADULTS (18-29)

Historically, young adults age 18 to 29 are the healthiest portion of the population. While some have chronic health conditions and require extensive or ongoing medical care, most do not. Young adult males rarely seek medical attention, while young adult females mostly use preventive care, generally for reproductive health issues.

Before Obamacare

Parents have been allowed to carry their young adult children on their health insurance plans up to age 24, as long as the child was still a dependent (for instance, a full-time student). Once a young adult left home and/or entered the workforce, it was up to them to obtain their own health insurance. Many young people enter the workforce as entry-level or minimum-wage workers, for whom health insurance is often not offered through their employer. Some are eligible for insurance but choose not to buy in, due to the cost and the fact that they perceive they do not need it. Many young adult women used free or sliding-scale clinics or the local health department to obtain gynecological preventive care and contraceptives.

With Obamacare

Individual mandates starting in 2014 will require most young adults to purchase health insurance. Requiring young, healthy adults to carry health insurance expands the pool of people who pay in, while not expanding the pool of people who collect benefits. The income this group is expected to generate will be used to partially fund the Medicaid and HIX program subsidies that will be taking care of the more seriously and chronically ill. This has been perceived as unfair by some, and so young, healthy adults will be allowed to purchase a catastrophic plan (see "Key Terms"), one that covers only emergencies and serious illnesses, rather than being required to purchase a more traditional plan that also covers primary care doctor visits and preventive care. It is expected that young adult females may tend to purchase plans with wider coverage.[19]

In March 2010, young adults became eligible to remain on their parents' medical plan up to age 26. The strict eligibility guidelines were also relaxed, and young adults no longer have to be full-time students, for instance, or live at home to qualify. However, if the parent doesn't have health insurance that includes dependents, the young adult can still purchase a low-cost plan that meets the federal government guidelines regarding preventive care. Starting in 2014, this process will be greatly simplified when the state HIX are introduced, and it will be easier to search for lower-cost options.

SENIOR CITIZENS (65+)

Since 1965, all Americans age 65 and older have been eligible for Medicare, which has given them access to medical care and has improved health care for the elderly overall and increased longevity. However, when Medicare was first implemented, the biggest worry was extended illness and longer hospital stays, and Medicare is designed to provide the most coverage in those situations. Health care today relies more on medication to combat illnesses and clinic-based procedures rather than hospital stays. Today's seniors can expect to lead longer, healthier lives, but problems with the original structure of the Medicare plan have created a situation where they pay higher out-of-pocket costs than most privately insured people when Medicare doesn't cover aspects of their health care. This has resulted in many insurance companies offering supplemental Medicare policies for individual purchase, thus increasing the amount that seniors ultimately pay for their health care.

Before Obamacare

Medicare has historically paid for 80 percent of medical bills, with senior patients being responsible for the other 20 percent. This opened the door for private health insurance companies to market supplemental policies, the coverage of which varies widely. Advances in the pharmaceutical field have led to more and more illnesses being treated with medication rather than a hospital stay, yet Medicare has limited drug coverage. As a result, out-of-pocket expenses for seniors have skyrocketed. The difference between what Medicare pays for drugs and what the drugs actually cost—a gap known as the "donut hole" (see "Key Terms")—has been the responsibility of the patient.

More and more seniors find themselves having to supplement their Medicare coverage with Medicaid (if their incomes are low) or private insurance. In 1997, the federal government came up with Medicare Part C, also known as the Medicare Advantage program. Under this program, consumers join an HMO or preferred provider organization (PPO), the government pays a lump sum per patient to the insurer, and out-of-pocket costs are eliminated or greatly reduced, depending on the plan chosen.

With Obamacare

Seniors 65 and older will not see their primary coverage change. Medicare Part D, which is prescription drug coverage, implemented in 2003, will be expanded in an effort to control pharmaceutical charges and close the donut hole. Private insurers will also have a cap on what they can charge for supplemental policies, thus capping rising premiums that now come with increased age. Medicare recipients will see no change in their benefits, other than the reduction of the donut hole. However, reductions have been proposed both in the amount Medicare Advantage plans are paid per patient and in reimbursements from the government to health care providers and facilities. Medicare cuts are a highly politicized issue, and it is difficult to predict what will happen to any proposal to cut Medicare spending. If cuts do go through, it is likely some physicians and private clinics will stop seeing Medicare patients, who will be forced to seek care elsewhere, possibly reducing the level of care received.

Proponents of Obamacare say Medicare spending cuts will reduce unnecessary costs (such as some costs paid out to hospitals and private insurance companies), and that this savings will help pay for the program overall. Opponents argue that doctors will stop accepting Medicare patients because of low reimbursement rates, hospitals will struggle, and individuals will have their options limited.

CHILDREN UNDER AGE 18

Parents of children under the age of 18 have had to face some hard choices over the past twenty years. Health care and health insurance premium costs have risen sharply, and some employers have elected to drop or limit coverage for dependents. The Medicaid program has been unavailable for most parents because they earn too much money. To fill the gap, in 1997 states partnered with the federal government to form SCHIP, which was designed to provide essential services for uninsured children and pregnant women who did not meet the financial eligibility requirements for Medicaid.

Before Obamacare

Parents of children under the age of 18 have historically had several choices regarding health insurance for their children. If the child was not covered by the parent's employer-offered plan or if the parent was unemployed, there were two programs available through their state: Medicaid and SCHIP. Children of working parents who made too much to qualify for Medicaid but not enough to purchase a private health plan ended up with SCHIP. In 2009, the program was expanded to provide funding to cover four million more children and pregnant women. Even with federal funding, though, SCHIP has been facing budget shortfalls in several states.

With Obamacare

Many parents will continue to insure their children through employer-offered health care plans. For those who don't have this option, though, Obamacare has expanded the Medicaid program to accept children and pregnant women whose family income is 133 percent or less of the federal poverty level. The SCHIP program has been expanded to include all uninsured children and pregnant women who are not covered by a private plan. Both Medicaid and SCHIP are administered by the states but are increasingly funded by the federal government.

As of 2010, certain preventive services for children and adolescents are also now mandated to be provided by all insurers, without having to pay a co-payment or co-insurance or meet a deductible (if the services are performed by an in-network provider). These include screening for a variety of health problems, including deafness, developmental difficulties, and autism, and all immunizations.[20]

PARENTS WITH CHILDREN OVER AGE 18

Most private insurance plans stopped covering children when they turned 18, unless they were full-time students, who could be covered until they turned 21. As more children started attending college, this age limit was raised to 24. For those not covered by their parents, Medicaid and SCHIP were unavailable unless the children were able to qualify on their own, and the requirements to qualify for these programs were extremely difficult to meet unless a female child was pregnant.

Before Obamacare

Parents of children over the age of 18 who were not students have had few options, especially if they are not able to cover their children on an employer-provided health insurance plan. Many of these young adults end up being uninsured. For those who want contraceptives or counseling or treatment for sexually transmitted diseases (STDs), local health departments or Planned Parenthood or other family planning clinics are low-cost options, but the range of services they offer is limited.

With Obamacare

Obamacare made several changes that were effective in 2010. Children with pre-existing conditions cannot be denied coverage under private plans. Children up to the age of 26 can be covered under their parents' medical insurance without the requirement of being full-time students. And insurance carriers can no longer abruptly cancel policies for minor reasons (this cancellation is called a "rescission"), nor can they put a cap on annual or lifetime benefits.

ADULT MALES

Male adults, especially those under the age of 30, have historically used fewer medical services than females. This is due in part to the fact that men do not bear children and also to the culturally ingrained idea that men should be so tough that they do not seek medical attention. Since Obamacare will require, starting in 2014, that all Americans have a health insurance plan of some sort, it is predicted that many young males between the ages of 18 and 30 will be insured for the first time.

Before Obamacare

Most male adults are either covered by their (or a spouse's) employer's health insurance plan or choose to go without health insurance. Primary care is rarely used by the uninsured, and in general, adult males seek care far less frequently than adult females. Urgent care for the uninsured is most often sought from local emergency rooms or urgent care clinics.

With Obamacare

Starting in 2014, uninsured adult males will be required to have health insurance—from an employer, by qualifying for Medicaid, or by purchasing a plan from their state's HIX. Certain preventive services for all adults are now mandated to be provided by all insurers, without having to pay a co-payment or co-insurance or meet a deductible (if they are done by an in-network provider). This includes screening for blood pressure, diabetes, obesity, STDs (including HIV), tobacco use, cholesterol, and depression, and all immunizations. Abdominal aortic aneurysm screening is also mandated for men.[21]

The Obamacare plan is counting on young males to purchase plans but use far fewer medical services. The presence of a large number of healthy people in the insurance pool helps subsidize care for those who need more services. Opposition to this inequity resulted in a compromise: Adults (male and female) up to age 30 may purchase a catastrophic plan that covers only serious illness or injury, rather than a comprehensive plan.

ADULT FEMALES

Female adults have historically used the health care system more than males, both for contraception and child bearing. After noticing that some women go to their gynecologist for primary care, insurance companies began to classify gynecologists as primary care providers, rather than specialists. This tends to give women more access to their gynecologist at a lower out-of-pocket cost but has also driven down reimbursement rates to gynecologists.

Before Obamacare

As with adult males, most insured adult females are currently covered under an employer-offered health insurance plan—either theirs or a family member's. Those who are not covered either qualify for Medicaid or remain uninsured. Any uninsured pregnant woman is guaranteed Medicaid for the duration of her pregnancy and aftercare. Uninsured adult women who are not pregnant tend to seek urgent care from emergency rooms or urgent care clinics, or seek preventive care from their local health department or clinics such as Planned Parenthood. In many cases, even women covered under a private insurance plan have had to pay for contraception out of pocket.

With Obamacare

Starting in 2014, uninsured adult females will be required to have health insurance—from their employer, by qualifying for Medicaid, or by purchasing a plan from their state's HIX. As with adult men, adult women under the age of 30 may opt to purchase a catastrophic plan.

Certain preventive services for women are mandated to be provided by all insurers, without having to pay a co-payment or co-insurance or meet a deductible (if they are done by an in-network provider). These include immunizations, mammograms, PAP tests, STD screening, and osteoporosis screening, and counseling for victims of domestic violence. For pregnant women, folic acid supplements, breast-feeding support, genetic testing, and other services are mandated.[22] Contraception is mandated to be covered for all adult females.

PEOPLE WITH MENTAL ILLNESS

One in four Americans has a diagnosable mental illness.[23] However, the mental health care system is underfunded and has been for many decades, leading to a general decline in the availability of mental health services. Most private insurance plans offer access to treatment and counseling centers, but the duration of covered treatment is often limited. People covered by Medicaid and the uninsured have few options.

Before Obamacare

States have cut more than $5 billion from their mental health services over the past four years.[24] Today, a person with a mental disability must either be covered by a private insurance plan offering mental health benefits, or try to seek help from a state-sponsored clinic. These clinics are not found in every state, due to funding cuts, and are overcrowded and unable to offer care to all those who need it. Most insurance plans strictly limit the amount of mental health treatment they will provide each year.

With Obamacare

Under Obamacare, the federal government will provide states with partial funding for mental health care. However, states are not required to accept these funds, and many states are choosing to opt out of providing mental health care to their residents. At this time, there are no penalties for the states if they do not offer mental health care.

WEALTHY ADULTS

Wealthy adults generally enjoy a high level of health insurance coverage.

Before Obamacare

Very few wealthy Americans are uninsured, and those that do not have insurance typically are able to pay for their health care. Most of the wealthy population is either employed or self-employed—or are covered under a family member's plan. Employed executives are sometimes covered under the same health insurance plan as all the other company employees, and are sometimes covered under higher-priced, high-end plans that offer a wider range of benefits. The wealthy self-employed are able to afford to purchase health insurance for themselves and their family.

With Obamacare

Wealthy Americans' insurance benefits will not change under Obamacare, but they will be affected by new taxes. Starting in 2014, individuals making more than $200,000 a year can expect to pay a higher Medicare tax. In 2018, there will also be an excise tax (up to 40 percent of the cost of the insurance plan)[25] if they elect to carry a high-end insurance plan. Proponents argue that it is only right for wealthier Americans to pay more because they can afford more, while opponents argue that these new taxes unfairly target the wealthy.

MIDDLE-CLASS ADULTS

Currently, most middle-class adults are working, and many have health insurance through their employers or through a working family member. However, as health insurance premiums have risen, many employers are picking up a smaller percentage of the cost. Payroll deductions for health insurance, especially to cover a whole family, have risen sharply for most middle-class Americans. Out-of-pocket costs for health care (co-pays, deductibles, benefit limits, and expenses that are not covered) have also risen in the past decade, as employers opt for plans with fewer features as a way to control costs.

Before Obamacare

The majority of middle-class Americans get their health insurance through their or a family member's employer. Some work for employers who do not offer a health insurance plan or who have dropped health care coverage for their employees as a cost-saving measure. In addition, changes in the makeup of the workforce mean a growing number of middle-class Americans are self-employed. Private individual plans are typically expensive for someone with a middle-class income. Some people therefore choose to purchase only catastrophic insurance plans or plans that offer a low level of coverage. Others go without health insurance. This has led to the creation of a large pool of people, estimated at thirty million, who earn too much to qualify for Medicaid but who cannot afford to purchase a private individual health insurance plan.

With Obamacare

With the expansion of Medicaid, the advent of state HIXs in 2014, and the mandate for companies with more than fifty employees to offer health insurance, most middle-class Americans will find an option for health insurance. Under the individual mandate, they must either be insured or pay a penalty (which is calculated on a sliding scale). The expansion of mandated services should help reduce out-of-pocket expenses, at least for some middle-class families.

Proponents of the plan point to data showing that an insured population is also a healthier population, and that by mandating health insurance for all, the United States will have a healthier working class, which will ultimately help drive health care costs down. Opponents say the individual mandate will place an undue economic burden on middle-class families.

IMPOVERISHED ADULTS

Historically, impoverished adults have qualified for Medicaid. Minimum-wage earners (sometimes referred to as the "working poor") have also sometimes been able to qualify for Medicaid, but often they do not. Medicaid programs and income guidelines vary from state to state.

Before Obamacare

Impoverished people cannot afford to purchase private individual health insurance plans. If they are employed, it is typically at a part-time and/or minimum-wage job that does not offer health insurance. Many people living at or below the official poverty line are covered under their states' Medicaid programs. But since qualifying requirements vary widely from state to state, a good number of impoverished adults are uninsured. They typically delay a visit to the doctor until their needs are urgent, and then tend to use public clinics and hospital emergency rooms for their medical care.

With Obamacare

Obamacare will raise the upper income limit to qualify for Medicaid in all states to 133 percent of the federal poverty level. After full implementation of Obamacare, it is estimated that there will be fifteen million more people able to get health care coverage through Medicaid. The benefits offered to current Medicaid recipients will not change. However, with potentially fifteen million more people in the system, the quality of care may decline and the time it takes to see a health care provider may increase. With some states opting out of the expanded Medicaid programs, the estimate of fifteen million people may be inflated.

SMALL-BUSINESS EMPLOYEES

Many small businesses (defined as businesses employing fewer than twenty-five people) currently do not offer medical benefits to their employees. Those that do have had to face the sharply rising costs of health insurance premiums in the past decade.

Before Obamacare

For employees who are covered by their employer, rising costs of health insurance premiums have sometimes pushed employers to offer plans with less coverage and more out-of-pocket costs. Employees of small businesses that do not offer health insurance have had to qualify for Medicaid, purchase an individual plan, or remain uninsured.

With Obamacare

Small-business owners are not mandated to provide health insurance for their employees. However, starting in 2014, small-business owners are being encouraged to offer insurance plans through tax rebates. If employers choose not to offer this benefit, some employees will qualify for Medicaid under the expanded guidelines. Others will be able to purchase a plan through the states' insurance exchanges. Either way, employees of small businesses are mandated to be covered by health insurance.

SMALL-BUSINESS OWNERS

Small businesses today are hurt by rising health care costs just as much as large businesses, but it is more difficult for them to absorb those losses. Numerous small and large businesses, in anticipation of the new law, have threatened to lay off a portion of their work force.[26] However, the employer mandate (see "Key Terms") to offer health insurance does not apply to businesses that employ fewer than fifty people.

Before Obamacare

Many small businesses choose to not insure their employees, because health insurance costs are high. Small businesses that do offer insurance have historically had to pay higher costs to insure their employees, as well as higher administrative costs associated with offering employee benefits, because their smaller size means they have less buying power.

With Obamacare

In 2014, small-business owners will be offered tax credits in exchange for offering their employees health insurance. Caps on the amount of profit health insurance companies can realize may eventually bring health care premiums down, as well. If the owners decide not to offer health insurance, their employees will be added to the pool of the uninsured who purchase a subsidized plan from their state's HIX (assuming they do not qualify for Medicaid). If the HIXs succeed, small businesses could realize financial benefits, again in the form of tax credits.

LARGE-BUSINESS EMPLOYEES

Large businesses (defined as businesses that employ more than twenty-five people) have traditionally offered health insurance as a part of their benefits packages. This is meant to attract and retain high-quality employees. Employee retention is important for large businesses, as employee training and administrative costs are typically higher for larger companies.

Before Obamacare

Historically, employees of large businesses have had health insurance benefits and paid only a small portion of the actual premiums, while the business itself picked up the rest. Many employees of large businesses also cover one or more family member though their employer's insurance plan. Rising health insurance premiums mean the employee's contribution to their health insurance, especially for family members, and out-of-pocket expenses have risen in the past decade.

Large businesses with many part-time employees and/or minimum-wage workers (such as McDonald's) sometimes offer mini-med insurance plans with very limited coverage.

With Obamacare

As of January 2014, if you work thirty hours a week or more and your employer has at least fifty full-time workers, they are required to offer a health insurance plan or pay a penalty. (Obamacare currently sets that fine at $2,000 per employee after the first thirty employees.) Caps on insurance benefits paid out per year and over a lifetime will be eliminated, and more mandated services may make health care services less expensive for some insured families.

Due to the elimination of mini-med insurance plans, the chances are greater that health care insurance will not be offered at large businesses with many part-time employees and/or minimum-wage workers. However, many minimum-wage employees of large businesses will be able to qualify for the expanded Medicaid program when the mini-med plans are eliminated.

LARGE-BUSINESS OWNERS

Large-business owners who supply health insurance benefits pay an additional one to one and a half dollars per hour to an employee's salary.[27] It is generally acknowledged that offering health insurance to full-time employees is part of the price of doing business in the United States today.

Before Obamacare

Most large businesses offer some form of health insurance to their employees, ranging from mini-med packages for minimum-wage employees to high-end plans for senior-level employees. Many companies also allow employees to cover family members and/or domestic partners under their employer's plan. The percentage of the plan's cost that the employer pays, and the coverage the plan offers, varies widely.

With Obamacare

As of January 2014, employers who have at least fifty full-time workers (employees who work thirty hours a week or more, on average) will be required to offer a health plan or pay a $2,000 fine per employee, not counting the first thirty employees. The insurance offered must cover at least 60 percent of the cost of benefits, and the employees' share may not be more than 9.5 percent of their income.[28]

Proponents of this employer mandate argue that implementing national standards, mandating health insurance for all Americans, and more closely regulating the insurance industry should eventually drive health insurance costs down. Opponents say the mandate on employers to provide health insurance will stifle economic growth by providing a disincentive for businesses to hire more people.

HEALTH INSURANCE COMPANIES

Insurance companies initially lobbied against Obamacare, but they ultimately supported it and continue to do so.[29] They stand to gain about thirty million new customers, most of whom are young and healthy.

Before Obamacare

To date, and up to 2014 and the opening of state HIXs, insurance companies have relied primarily on business generated by large companies purchasing health insurance for their employees. In 1997, with the advent of Medicare Part C, they were able to expand into the Medicare Advantage market. Additionally, they were able to sell individual plans to the self-employed and unemployed.

Insurance companies have been able to charge whatever price they feel the market will bear for health insurance premiums, and decide what services they will and will not cover (subject to a variety of state laws).

With Obamacare

Obamacare requires health insurers in the individual and small-group market to spend 80 percent of their premiums (after subtracting taxes and regulatory fees) on medical costs. The corresponding figure for large groups is 85 percent. Health insurance companies may no longer refuse to pay for pre-existing conditions or impose lifetime or annual spending caps on insured persons or families. In addition, many types of services are mandated to be provided with no out-of-pocket costs to the insured.

With the implementation of the individual and employer mandates, insurance companies will see an influx of new customers, many of whom will have their bills paid or subsidized by the federal government. Reimbursements to insurance companies for Medicare Advantage plans had been scheduled for cuts but no longer are. However those cuts could be reinstated at any time.

PHARMACEUTICAL COMPANIES

The lobby for the Pharmaceutical Research and Manufacturing Association (PhRMA) has supported Obamacare. Pharmaceutical companies agreed to provide billions of dollars in subsidies to expand the Medicare Part D program, thus helping with efforts to close the Medicare donut hole. These billions are predicted to be offset by the addition of thirty million potential new customers.

Before Obamacare

Pharmaceutical companies are very profitable. Some of these profits are used to fund research and development, which often takes place in the United States in order to comply with Food and Drug Administration (FDA) regulations. The resulting drugs are marketed in countries where drug prices are not regulated (such as the United States), and countries where drug prices are regulated (such as most of Europe). In the countries with unregulated prices, drugs typically cost much more than in the countries with regulated prices. The drug companies say these higher costs help to fund more research and development.

With Obamacare

Drug prices will continue to be unregulated in the United States. The influx of thirty million insured Americans may offer a significant boost to pharmaceutical companies' revenues. Eventually, some analysts expect that in addition to the subsidies provided to Medicare Part D recipients, pharmaceutical companies will also have to offer some sort of discount or rebate to patients in the expanded Medicaid programs.[30] However, this is not expected to greatly impact the bottom line for pharmaceutical companies. Still, according to an official PhRMA website, the industry is wary of what impact the new law will have.[31]

Obamacare Timeline[32]

March 2010: President Barack Obama signs the Patient Protection and Affordable Care Act into law.

July 2010: A government-run high-risk pool provides insurance for adults with pre-existing conditions until all insurance plans provide this coverage in January 2014.

September 2010: Children under age 18 can no longer be rejected by insurers because they have a pre-existing health condition. Children up to age 26 can be insured as dependents and covered by their parents' insurance policy. Insurance plans can no longer impose a lifetime limit on a policyholder's benefits. Insurance plans can no longer impose an annual limit on a policyholder's benefits (a phase-in period begins, with a total ban effective January 2014). Insurance companies can no longer terminate policies they deem too costly due to consumers' health. A maximum tax credit of 35 percent of the cost of insurance premiums is available to small businesses with twenty-five or fewer employees.[33]

January 2014: Medicaid expands to cover people with an income level of up to 133 percent of the federal poverty line in every state. (A handful of states, including Texas and Florida, have announced that they will not go along with this part of Obamacare, and because of a 2012 Supreme Court ruling, the federal government cannot punish them financially for their noncompliance.)[34] Health insurance exchanges (HIXs) selling insurance to individuals and small businesses open for business nationwide. If a state does not set one up—some, like Florida and Alaska, have announced they won't—the federal government will create and run it for them. An individual mandate tax will be instituted—Americans who do not obtain health insurance expose themselves to a maximum penalty of $285 per year. Adults age 18 and older can no longer be rejected for insurance because of a pre-existing health condition. Young adults under age 30 can buy low-priced catastrophic insurance through the HIXs. Insurance plans must cover "essential health benefits" (approved preventive care and screening covered as of September 2010). A maximum tax credit of 50 percent of the cost of insurance premiums is available to small businesses with twenty-five or fewer employees.

January 2015: The individual mandate tax increases—Americans who do not obtain health insurance are subject to a maximum penalty of $975. An Independent Payment Advisory Board (IPAB) can begin making recommendations to cut Medicare spending.

January 2016: The individual mandate tax increases—Americans who do not obtain health insurance may be subject to a maximum penalty of $2,085.

January 2017: HIXs can be expanded to include large businesses with more than one hundred employees, if a state chooses to let them in.

January 2018: IPAB's recommendations about Medicare's budget can be implemented. A tax on high-end insurance plans begins.

Key Terms

catastrophic plan   A lower-cost health insurance plan that covers only hospitalization—typically, with a high deductible before coverage kicks in. Under Obamacare, catastrophic plans will be allowed only for adults under the age of 30.

COBRA   The Consolidated Omnibus Budget Reconciliation Act, passed in 1986, ensures that people who lose their group medical benefits (for reasons such as job loss) can continue to purchase the plan through their former employer for a maximum of eighteen months. The employer does not have to contribute anything toward the cost of the insurance.

employer mandate   The requirement that businesses with fifty or more employees offer their full-time workers a health insurance plan.

health insurance exchange (HIX)   The marketplace where private insurers offer health care plans. The plans may be different from state to state but must be consistent with the requirements of Obamacare. The exchanges can be available in some areas through walk-in stores.

individual mandate   Obamacare requires all Americans to be covered by a health insurance policy or be subject to a fine. As of 2014 that fine will be up to $285 per year. By 2020, the fine will be as high as $2,085.

Medicaid   Health care coverage for impoverished Americans jointly funded by the states and the federal government.

Medicare   A health care plan for senior citizens (age 65 or older) and disabled Americans. Under Obamacare, Medicare coverage is not expected to change in any significant way.

Medicare donut hole   Medicare Part D covered the cost of prescription drugs when they exceed a certain accumulated value. If people didn't purchase a supplementary policy to cover Part D, they'd have a "donut hole" in their insurance plan until they reached the value threshold.

mini-med plan   Basic health care plans that cover a minimum number of doctor visits, sometimes offered by large companies whose employees earn minimum wage. Mini-med plans will no longer be allowed under Obamacare.

Patient Protection and Affordable Care Act (PPACA)   Otherwise known as Obamacare, a comprehensive health care overhaul plan signed into law by President Barack Obama on March 23, 2010.

pre-existing condition   Currently, many insurance plans will not accept new clients who have a health condition, including a mental illness. Obamacare will do away with this practice by 2014.

public option   A government-run health insurance plan to run alongside private plans and funded by premiums rather than government money. Obamacare is not a public option plan, but states have the choice to offer it to their citizens. See **single payer**.

SCHIP   State Children's Health Insurance Program, funded in part by the federal government, offers a health care program for children under the age of 18 from needy families.

single payer A system by which one payer, such as the federal government, collects fees and covers all payouts for all medical costs for all citizens. Single payer is not and never was part of Obamacare.

universal health care A system offering government-funded and administered health care for all citizens, with equal services to wealthy and impoverished citizens. The United Kingdom is an example of a country that has a universal health care law. Obamacare is not a universal health care law; it is a universal health insurance law.

Recommended Reading

Jonathan Gruber and Nathan Schreiber, *Health Care Reform: What It Is, Why It's Necessary, How It Works* **(Hill and Wang, 2011)**

The authors of this book argue against Obamacare, stating that a mounting avalanche of misinformation about the bill is confusing millions of Americans and will impede their ability to make wise and thoughtful decisions regarding their health care choices over the next few years.

Lawrence R. Jacobs and Theda Skocpol, *Health Care Reform and American Politics: What Everyone Needs to Know* **(Oxford University Press, 2010)**

Jacobs and Skocpol, two experts on politics and health care reform, detail the politics and infighting that occurred before the final passage of the ground-breaking bill. They show how various lobbying groups, as well as the Tea Party, influenced the final wording of the bill. Also detailed is what the new law can do for everyday Americans, how much it will ultimately cost, and how it will be funded.

Betsy McCaughey, *Decoding the Obama Health Law: What You Need to Know* **(Paperless Publishing, 2012)**

Constitutional scholar, patient advocate, and former lieutenant governor of New York state, McCaughey presents an easy read, detailing many of the faults, hidden costs, and bizarre add-ons to the Obamacare bill. Her book is biased toward the right but still brings salient points to the forefront, resulting in an informative and in-depth read.

T. R. Reid, *The Healing of America: A Global Quest for Better, Cheaper, and Fairer Health Care* **(Penguin, 2010)**

Reid visits industrialized democracies around the world—France, Britain, Germany, Japan, and others—to provide a tour of successful, affordable universal health care systems. Now updated with new statistics and a plain-English explanation of the 2010 health care reform bill, *The Healing of America* explains, in straightforward terms, the state of health care in our country, and around the world, with a strong appreciation of the universal health care model.

Staff of the *Washington Post, Landmark: The Inside Story of America's New Health Care Law and What It Means for Us All* **(PublicAffairs, 2010)**

In this book, the staff of the *Washington Post* present an objective and informational overview of the political process that led to the signing of the Patient Protection and Affordable Care Act, complete with a description of the rancorous, divisive arguments that preceded the passage of Obamacare. The authors also examine the new law's impact on individuals, families, doctors and other health care professionals, and insurers.

Nate Tate, *Obamacare Survival Guide* **(Humanix Books, 2012)**

Tate's book, though obviously not a pro-Obamacare missive, is written with a clear and concise voice. Tate tries to simplify the law and present it in simple terms, and covers such subjects as Medicare cuts, how the law will affect various demographics, new protections for the uninsured, new taxes and budget cuts implemented to pay for it, and a multitude of other issues.

Ron Taylor, *ObamaCare: A Patient Protection and Affordable Care Act Survival Handbook for Consumers and Employers* **(Amazon eBook, 2013)**

In this book, Taylor outlines the benefits and pitfalls included in Obamacare. He explains how portions of the bill will affect various American demographics, explaining that those who do not take the time and trouble to research and understand the intricacies of the bill will ultimately be exploited through their own ignorance of the facts and opportunities being presented to them.

http://en.wikipedia.org/wiki/Obamacare

This excellent and exhaustive Wikipedia entry details the history behind the Patient Protection and Affordable Care Act, the politics and infighting leading to the passing of the bill, and how Obamacare will affect different segments of the population, including the timeline by which it will be implemented.

http://Obamacarefacts.com/affordablecareact-summary.php

This site contains the most detailed collection of facts about the bill itself and how it will affect different Americans, organized by demographic groups. The site's authors say it is the most factual representation of the bill because it breaks down Obamacare into its simplest form. Every title and every section of the Affordable Care Act is packed with details (even the condensed version of the bill is over nine hundred pages long), and this site offers a summary of the whole act.

http://healthcare.gov

This is an interactive site aimed at helping Americans understand how the law will affect them personally. You can find the health insurance best suited to your needs, whether it's private insurance for individuals, families, and small businesses, or public programs. It was created to help consumers understand the health insurance reform law.

http://cciio.cms.gov/

The Center for Consumer Information and Insurance Oversight (CCIIO) is charged with helping implement the provisions of the Affordable Care Act that relate to private health insurance. This website contains information on government regulations that pertain to health insurance companies, including health insurance exchanges, insurance market reforms, and consumer rights when dealing with health insurance companies.

Endnotes

1. Nick J. Tate, *Obamacare Survival Guide* (West Palm Beach, Florida: Humanix Books, 2012).

2. "Social Security History: The Evolution of Medicare," Social Security Administration, accessed April 11, 2013 www.ssa.gov/history/corningchap3.html.

3. Ibid.

4. "Dwight D. Eisenhower," The American Presidency Project, accessed April 11, 2013 www.presidency.ucsb.edu/ws/index.php?pid=10399.

5. "Nixon's Plan for Health Reform, In His Own Words," Kaiser Health News, September 3, 2009 www.kaiserhealthnews.org/stories/2009/september/03/nixon-proposal.aspx.

6. Max Fisher, "Here's a Map of the Countries That Provide Universal Health Care (America's Still Not on It)," *The Atlantic*, June 28, 2012 www.theatlantic.com/international/archive/2012/06/heres-a-map-of-the-countries-that-provide-universal-health-care-americas-still-not-on-it/259153.

7. "Estimates for the Insurance Coverage Provisions of the Affordable Care Act Updated for the Recent Supreme Court Decision," Congressional Budget Office, July 24, 2012 www.cbo.gov/publication/43472.

8. Chapin White and Amanda E. Lechner, "State Benefit Mandates and National Health Reform," *National Institute for Health Care Reform*, No. 8 (February 2012) www.familiesusa.org/assets/pdfs/NIHCR_StateMandates.pdf.

9. Ian Urbina, "Beyond Beltway, Health Debates Turn Hostile," *New York Times*, August 7, 2009 www.nytimes.com/2009/08/08/us/politics/08townhall.html.

10. Daniel Fisher, "Supreme Court Upholds Obamacare: What It Means, What Happens Next," *Forbes*, June 28, 2012 www.forbes.com/sites/danielfisher/2012/06/28/supreme-court-upholds-healthcare-law-what-it-means.

11. "Employer Health Benefits 2012 Annual Survey," The Henry J. Kaiser Family Foundation, September 11, 2012 http://ehbs.kff.org/.

12. "2012 HHS Poverty Guidelines," U.S. Department of Health and Human Services, last modified February 9, 2012 http://aspe.hhs.gov/poverty/12poverty.shtml#thresholds.

13. Ibid.

14. Sarah Kliff, "The Obamacare Exchanges Are Important. Who Runs Them Isn't," *Washington Post*, December 14, 2012 www.washingtonpost.com/blogs/wonkblog/wp/2012/12/14/the-Obamacare-exchanges-are-important-who-runs-them-isnt.

15. Karen E. Klein, "Advice for Small Employers Confused by Obamacare," *Bloomberg/Businessweek*, March 28, 2013 www.businessweek.com/articles/2013-03-28/advice-for-small-employers-confused-by-obamacare.

16. "2012 HHS Poverty Guidelines," U.S. Department of Health and Human
    Services, last modified February 9, 2012
    http://aspe.hhs.gov/poverty/12poverty.shtml#thresholds.

17. Frequently Asked Questions: COBRA Continuation Health Coverage
    U.S. Department of Labor, accessed April 11, 2013
    www.dol.gov/ebsa/faqs/faq-consumer-cobra.html.

18. "Illegal Immigration to the United States," Wikipedia,
    accessed April 14, 2013
    http://en.wikipedia.org/wiki/Illegal_immigration_to_the_United_States.

19. Lawrence R. Jacobs and Theda Skocpol, *Health Care Reform and
    American Politics: What Everyone Needs to Know* (New York:
    Oxford University Press, 2010).

20. "Preventive Services Covered Under the Affordable Care Act," Health
    Care.gov, last modified September 27, 2012
    www.healthcare.gov/news/factsheets/2010/07/preventive-services-list.
    html#CoveredPreventiveServicesforChildren.

21. Ibid.

22 Ibid.

23 Erin Mershon, "Will 'Obamacare' Fill the Gaps in Our Mental Health
    System?" *National Journal*, December 28, 2012
    www.nationaljournal.com/healthcare/will-obamacare-fill-the-gaps-in-our-
    mental-health-system-20121228.

24. Ibid.

25. "Patient Protection and Affordable Care Act," Wikipedia,
    accessed April 11, 2013
    http://en.wikipedia.org/wiki/Patient_Protection_and_Affordable_Care_Act.

26. "Papa John's Obamacare Stance Cost Company Its Reputation: Study," *Huffington Post*, last modified December 4, 2012 www.huffingtonpost.com/2012/12/03/papa-johns-obamacare_n_2233525.html.

27. Joe Hadzima, "Starting Up: Practical Advice for Entrepreneurs," accessed April 11, 2013 http://web.mit.edu/e-club/hadzima/how-much-does-an-employee-cost.html.

28. Karen E. Klein, "Advice for Small Employers Confused by Obamacare," *Bloomberg/Businessweek*, March 28, 2013 www.businessweek.com/articles/2013-03-28/advice-for-small-employers-confused-by-obamacare.

29. Kimberly J. Kockler, "What U.S. Health Care Consumers Can Expect Next," Timesleader.com, February 19, 2013 http://timesleader.com/stories/What-US-health-care-consumers-can-expect-next-COMMENTARY-Kimberly-J-Kockler,229685.

30. Nick J. Tate, *Obamacare Survival Guide* (West Palm Beach, Florida: Humanix Books, 2012).

31. Tom Norton, "Obamacare After November 6th: Trouble for Pharma?" PharmExec.com, October 24, 2012 http://blog.pharmexec.com/2012/10/24/obamacare-after-nov-6th-trouble-for-pharma.

32. "Patient Protection and Affordable Care Act," Wikipedia, accessed April 11, 2013 http://en.wikipedia.org/wiki/Patient_Protection_and_Affordable_Care_Act.

33. Ibid.

34. http://aspe.hhs.gov/poverty/12poverty.shtml.

CPSIA information can be obtained at www.ICGtesting.com
Printed in the USA
BVOW04s0952300913

332496BV00001B/9/P